THE MINISTRY
TO THE
IMPRISONED

Joan Campbell, S.P.

D1716077

THE LITURGICAL PRESS
Collegeville, Minnesota 56321

To
Fr. Richard Stohr,
who first involved me in detention ministry,
and to
my cousin Kathleen,
who is always there . . . .

Cover design by Ann Blattner. Photo by Seventy Times Seven, published by Catholic Charities, Kansas City, Kansas. Other photos courtesy of George T. Kruse; used with permission.

4	5	6	7	8	9

Contents

Preface

I invite you to come with me inside the walls of a prison or a jail to see what Jesus meant when he asked us to visit him in prison. Sometimes we might prefer the "out of sight—out of mind" approach to incarceration. But Jesus is clearly there in the person of the prisoners, the poorest of the poor, society's outcasts needing to respond to God's unconditional love, even in this dehumanizing environment.

Given the circumstances of their lives, prisoners will appreciate your visit, your walking with them in the difficult journey of this time in their lives.

Since there are so many types of jails and prisons, my descriptions in this booklet are general. Hopefully, local people will introduce you to a particular facility. Given the structure of the correction system, *The Ministry to the Imprisoned* provides some background to help you feel more comfortable. Resources are listed to support your ministry, whether you choose to visit prisoners in an ongoing way inside or outside the walls.

Unfortunately, while the harvest of prisoners is great and while the rising crime rate is getting greater, in this ministry the laborers are few. Fortunately, however, the Church continues to respond to the needs of prisoners and in many dioceses has established centers or programs to help non-professionals work with the imprisoned. These are challenges to any response to the gospel message, but meeting Christ in the person of the prisoner can be a source of great personal growth. Journeying with them puts a person in touch with his or her own vulnerability, strengths, and peace and joy in the Lord.

I would like to thank those who contributed to, read, or critiqued the manuscript, namely, the chaplains, volunteers, and inmates in the Archdiocese of San Francisco, Ms. Kathy Carey, Mrs. Lorraine Castle, Br. Derek Ford, S.S.F., Br. Bill Farrell, S.M., Fr. Enzie Lagattuta, Sr. Anne Marie Raftery, O.F.M., Ms. Carol Ann Richlie, and Dr. Timothy McCarthy. I am also most grateful to Mrs. Irene Carpoff for typing the manuscript.

Joan Campbell, S.P.

Introduction

He came to Nazareth where he had grown up and went according to his custom into the synagogue on the sabbath day. He stood up to read and was handed a scroll of the prophet Isaiah. He unrolled the scroll and found the passage where it was written:

"The Spirit of the Lord is upon me,
  because he has anointed me
    to bring good tidings to the poor.

He has sent me to proclaim liberty to captives
  and recovery of sight to the blind
    to let the oppressed go free,
      and to proclaim a year acceptable to the Lord."

Isa 61:1-2

Rolling up the scroll, he handed it back to the attendant and sat down, and the eyes of all in the synagogue looked intently upon him. He said to them,
"Today this scripture passage is fulfilled in your hearing."

1

"I was in prison and you visited me . . ."
(Matt 25:36)

Jesus showed that he wanted to be taken seriously when he added to the above mandate: "When you refused to help the least of these my brothers, you were refusing to help me" (Matt. 26:45). Perhaps you are already involved in some type of ministry to the needy or the oppressed, but I would invite you to seriously consider the possibility of responding to the gospel call to help people who are incarcerated.

Many of us have grown up seeing family and friends involved in parish activities and in helping the poor, the sick, and the aged, but perhaps we have not been as exposed to the possible ministries to those in jail or prison. As a senior in high school I remember trying to decide whether God wanted me to be a nun or a policewoman. I decided on the former, never realizing that eventually I would be involved in both. For twenty-five years I was a teacher or a principal and received the direct "call" to prison ministry through an invitation by Fr. Richard Stohr at Monroe Prison in Washington. It was on-the-job training with Father Stohr modelling the type of caring and genuine connecting with the inmates that is so vital in this ministry. I soon began to appreciate the personalities of the individuals and to respond to their particular spiritual needs. After Monroe I worked with juvenile delinquents in Seattle and then with adults in other prisons in the state. When

I studied detention ministry in preparation for a full-time commitment, many of my Sisters, parishioners, and family members were at first concerned for my safety, concerned about the loss to the Catholic schools, and for some, even concerned about this ministry being a waste of time.

As a full-time detention chaplain, it is an inspiration to me to see how supportive these friends have become—many of whom are involved by daily prayer and other types of inclusion in the ministry. A few areas of involvement that I have seen in the United States and Canada include: St. Vincent de Paul Society offering financial support as well as individual members facilitating one-on-one visiting and religious services; volunteers working in jails as librarians, beauticians, and tutors, and in leading art projects, sports, and singing groups; persons with counseling background offering pastoral counseling; Eucharistic ministers providing Communion services; and others helping with religious services and retreats. The possibilities are truly extensive and those who have responded to the call have found it very rewarding.

2

Christians in Prison

The stories of the Old Testament unfold for us God's continual response to the needs of the poor and the oppressed as well as God's bringing them out of slavery. The prophets were continually echoing the cries of the oppressed and the voiceless, crying out for their dignity, human rights, and freedom.

In the New Testament, Jesus modeled a life of caring for the poor and the outcasts. My favorite story illustrating the compassion of Jesus is that of the adulterous woman (John 8:1-12). I always use this story with those who are incarcerated as Jesus' response toward them. He also challenged the systems of society to the point of dying on the cross, a victim of legalism and false societal norms. A suggestion to anyone interested in detention ministry is to read the gospel sections which relate the story of Jesus as a prisoner (Matt. 26:28; Mark 14:16; Luke 22:24; John 17:20). These sections are also good for dialogue or homilies with those in jail to illustrate the humanness of Jesus—sweating blood with fear when arrested, the indignities of his "booking" process, the unfairness of Pilate, the pain of his mother and friends, the injustices of the system. There is hope in that a fellow prisoner, crucified next to him, was one of the first to join Jesus in heaven.

Throughout the ages saints have been in prison for a variety of reasons. Prayerful reflection should be given to St. Paul's letters from prison: Philippians, Colossians, Philemon, Ephesians, and also to his experiences as related in the Acts of the Apostles. J. L. Houlden in *Paul's Letters from Prison* illustrates how "it is characteristic of Paul that in commending virtue he should appeal to the person and work of Christ—not to some saying or deed of his lifetime, but rather to his whole action in becoming man and dying a death which effected the reconciliation of man to God."[1] He shows how Paul dealt with incarceration, valued those who ministered to him, and used the time of incarceration to minister to others.

We are admonished by St. Paul to "be mindful of prisoners as if sharing their imprisonment" (Heb 13:3).

Other saints whose prison experiences can be an inspiration to us are:

• St. Joan of Arc who after saving France was captured and burned as a "heretic" by the English (died with word "Jesus" on her lips).

• St. Agnes who was beheaded because she insisted on her virginity.

• St. Vincent of Sargasso whose jailer was converted witnessing his torture for the faith.

• St. Maximilian Kolbe who was slowly starved to death in a German concentration camp after taking the place of another prisoner with a family.

• St. Blaise who, as a bishop, while en route to prison cured a child of a disease of the throat.

• St. Margaret Clitherow who was crushed under unbearable weights over a sharp rock for harboring "fugitive" priests.

• St. Benjamin, a deacon who died, after untold tortures, for preaching.

• St. Thomas More, patron of lawyers, who was imprisoned and executed for treason because he refused to endorse the divorce of England's Henry VIII.

• St. Francis of Assisi who, during a time of imprisonment at an early age, opted for a life of radical poverty in Christ's name.[2]

Others who wrote about their experiences in jail or prison were:

• John Henry Abbott wrote vividly of his prison experience in *In the Belly of the Beast*.[3] From his cell to the other sections of maximum security, Abbott puts us clearly in touch with intense feelings and depravation in an unnatural world of monotony and dehumanization.

• Jerry Graham relates through *Where Flies Don't Land* how being in and out of jail since age fourteen earned him the title "incorrigible criminal" by age thirty-eight.[4] Until he responded to God's love in his life, he found himself bound by drugs, booze, and crime.

• In *Prayers from Prison* the famous German martyr Dietrich Bonhoeffer reveals the richness of his spirituality during the desperate context of his life in prison from Christmas 1943 to Christmas 1944.[5] Even in the despicable role of a prisoner, he made of his life a liturgy and through his prayers developed a Christian community.

• Benjamin E. Chavis, one of the Wilmington Ten, captured his experience in *Psalms From Prison*.[6]

Persons who were models in visiting prisoners were:

• Our Lady of Sorrows who followed her Son to the foot of the cross.

• St. Vincent de Paul who was noted for visiting the poor in prison.

• Mother Emilie Gamelin who visited political prisoners in Canada.

• Pope John Paul II who visited Mehmet Ali Agca, the man who shot him.

One of the principal works of the Society of St. Vincent de Paul throughout the world is ministry to prisoners while incarcerated and upon release. In the spring 1833 the young college professor Frederick Ozanam encouraged some of his college students to get interested in social issues. From among these students he started the Conferences of St. Vincent de Paul, named after the French saint whose apostolate was protecting the poor, the sick, and the incarcerated through charitable works. "This was the first Catholic organization whose lay apostolate has a universal and permanent existence."[7] At the centennial of the foundation of the society, there were some 13,800 conferences with 750,000 members. In several dioceses in the United States and throughout the world, the society provides funding for full-time chaplains in corrections, for religious services programs, for training of volunteers, and for volunteers to serve this ministry.

3

Detention Ministry in the United States

In the United States punishment of offenders was first modelled on the often inhumane forms of punishment used in the Old World. Public executions, multiple hangings, stocks, torturing and whipping were not only signs of Puritan righteousness but also provided social outings for spectators.

On October 25, 1829, the Eastern State Penitentiary opened its doors in Pennsylvania to "receive the wayward and bring them to God."[9] The world's first penitentiary was a uniquely American experiment supported by Benjamin Franklin, Dr. Benjamin Rush, and other God-fearing Quakers looking for a humane alternative to punishment.

The program designed by the Pennsylvania Prison Society was based on the monastic tradition of silence, daily prayer, and absolute isolation (individual cells). The basis for reform was daily Bible reading and occasional visits from carefully screened Christian men. Societal pressures, over-crowding, and the nature of the sociopathic personality proved this system of reform ineffective.

Catholic Church Involvement

Since the early days of our country, the Church has been involved in advocacy for the incarcerated and in their pastoral care. In more recent years there have also been official pastoral statements, such as The Pastoral Statement on Criminal Justice by the Catholic Bishops of New York State in 1983. Our country has a history of providing Catholic and Protestant chaplains for federal and state facilities. A few cities and counties, such as New York, Cleveland, Bexar County, San Antonio, Texas; and Hanis County, Houston, Texas, provide for a Catholic chaplaincy in their facilities.

In more recent years there is a trend toward a diocesan coordination of detention ministry in all facilities housing adults and/or juveniles. Through this effort coordination programs are developed for involvement of chaplains and volunteers in direct ministry in the facilities, to their families outside the facilities, in advocacy for issues related to the incarcerated and for educational programs related to the needs of the incarcerated. It is hoped that with expanded chaplaincy programs and increased volunteer opportunities available, today, more people will become involved in ministry to the incarcerated.

For those who are newly incarcerated or those serving life terms, there is a need for support as they cope with their imprisonment. Easily 90 percent of those in prison and jail will be released; thus, we need to help with rehabilitative efforts in the facilities whether they be spiritually based, or whether they involve other programs such as Alcoholics Anonymous or Narcotics Anonymous, halfway houses, job procurement, etc.

4

Jail House Blues

My First Trip to "The Pen"

When I was in grade school, the juvenile facility in Seattle was across the street from a friend's house, so we sometimes visited the youths through the fence when they were allowed outside. Many in the facility were awaiting foster-home placement. While I had been through a local police station when visiting the sheriff, a friend of the family in a small town years before, I had never been inside a prison.

My first trip to "the pen" was at the invitation of Fr. Richard Stohr, chaplain at Monroe Prison, to help with religious services on Friday evenings and weekends. For my initial visit Father had prepared all the preliminary paperwork, security clearance, and administrative documentation to permit me to enter the prison with him. He suggested that after a couple of weeks I would go through the badging procedure (fingerprinting, pictures taken, etc.) if I could accompany him on a more regular basis.

I don't remember fearing for my safety in the prison as much as feeling powerless in the complexity of the system. We passed through an area with families and friends waiting for a short visit with a loved one. The area was charged with emotion: fear, confusion, and uncertain anticipation of what the visit would hold. I would have preferred staying with the visitors as their suffering was so great. Once inside the many locked doors, gates, and passageways, I was in the middle of an entirely self-contained city. Wanting to take it all in, I tried to stare inconspicuously without being obvious. I was clearly aware that I was in the prison by choice and the residents of this "city" were not.

On the way to the chapel area, Father Stohr explained the various classification areas to me. We passed the infirmary, the dining room, the laundry, the education building, and finally the softball area in the yard. The men in the passageways and yard were enjoying some free time from their cells and were permitted to come to the chapel if they wished. Some areas were locked because of the charge (types of crimes) or for protective custody of the inmates. Given appropriate behavior within the institution, most inmates had some time away from work or from their cells to be in the yard or to attend programs such as church services.

I'll never forget the faces on those men: young, alert, outgoing, and so grateful to see us. When we reached the chapel, we discovered how eager they were to help Father Stohr prepare for Mass; some had even made colorful flowers for the altar. After the initial greetings and "checking me out," a sense of trust quickly developed and their stories began to unfold. While a few considered their lives "on hold" during time in "the pen," most were interested in looking at their lives to consider how they might use their time productively while incarcerated and prepare for their return to society. It was in those evenings in the chapel that I really came to hear clearly the words of the Lord, "I was in prison, and you visited me" (Matt. 25:36). In the weeks that followed I understood what Jesus meant by "visited me" in the context of pastoral presence; that is, pastoral care.

When I started visiting Monroe Prison, I went to see what I could do for its ministry. I asked the same questions I had asked in other ministries: What could I bring? What could I give? What could I accomplish? How would I do? My days at Monroe taught me the essence of ministry. Never before had I prayed so hard or considered myself walking in with Our Lord and finding him there. Soon I was not looking for things to bring in or preparing lesson plans. Rather, I experienced the tender love, mercy, forgiveness, and compassion of Jesus manifesting itself through the pain of these people. The religious question is the essential one that faces the incarcerated in their desperate and powerless situation. I came to realize the strength of the message of the cross—that God accepts each of us with no strings attached. This leaves us free to be the fully human person that God created us to be no matter what our circumstances. I came to see Our Lord's presence in and through me in a very real way as I accompanied these men on their journey. This indeed, rather than "How did it go?", was my reward. Prison is not a place where we go to see things accomplished or to see people "saved." We come to see that Christ already lived to show us how to live, that he died to save us and to promote the process for redemption. In prison we can get in touch with our insecurities, our hurts, and anything in our lives that is an obstacle to that redemptive process. We can really experience the power of reconciliation in our lives. What a blessing to be a chaplain or a volunteer in this setting where Our Lord is so present.

Juvenile Facility Experience

That spring I was asked to visit the juvenile facility in Seattle since there was no Catholic presence there. In Monroe I had teamed with Father Stohr, so I felt that I should have more preparation to do something "on my own." Thus, I spent the summer in a chaplaincy training program (Clinical Pastoral Education) at Shelton Prison.

That fall I found the juvenile setting very different from life in prison. The youth were younger than I expected and in for serious charges (many prostitutes were nine, ten, or eleven years old). At one point there were five boys, fifteen or younger, charged with murder. Drugs, sex, and violent acts were very lucrative for the youth so there was little motivation to change. Unrest in life and uncertainty in how to "beat the system" were so prevalent that it was a challenge to develop a level of trust. Most youths had gang or street connections and were used to a life of being used or abused. It was hard for them to believe that someone really cared. While the goals were the same, developing a pastoral presence took on new dimensions.

Adult Jails

The transient quality of time in jail makes visiting there similar to that in juvenile facilities. Persons are newly arrested and waiting trial for breaking federal, state, or county laws. Some are sentenced to up to one year county time. Most jails are considerably overcrowded and programming is difficult or nonexistent because of lack of space. Similar to prisons, jails are generally quite self-contained with various basic services. But in a jail more people are in a smaller building with several to a cell. A small-town jail might even be combined with the local police station. In a large city over one thousand inmates may be in the jail. The average daily population of the Los Angeles men's central jail was eight thousand in 1986, and throughout the country 274,444 inmates were in jails of various jurisdictions.[10] Large jail populations were under court order to improve one or more conditions of confinement. The United States has approximately twenty-five per one hundred thousand persons incarcerated.

Jail House Blues

Who is in prison and/or jail today? People in jail come from our neighborhoods, parishes, and schools. We read their alleged stories in the newspapers. For the most part, those in jail could not afford bail or for other complex societal reasons could not be released on their own recognizance. The percentage of minorities, mentally ill, and younger persons in jail increases annually. Because of overcrowding, persons with less serious offenses are usually cited out (released without booking) or released early, leaving perpetrators of more serious crimes locked up. Some of the poor remain in jail because they cannot afford bail. The majority of crimes committed are alcohol or drug related.

Many persons in jail have sociopathic tendencies and behaviors. They become self-centered, antisocial, manipulative, and amoral. In addition to having a poor self-image, they have difficulty with realistic or value-centered goals. Personal insecurities, inconsistencies in relationships, and lack of support from significant others lead to feelings of hurt, mistrust, anger, fear, guilt, denial, and depression—even suicidal ideations and tendencies. We must not label persons in jail. In fact, we often see these tendencies in people who are not incarcerated, but it is important to be aware of addictive and sociopathic problems, since they can be found in prisoners. An excellent book to show the purest of the incarcerated sociopathic personality is S. Michaud's *The Only Living Witness.*[11] *Games Criminals Play*[12] by Bud Allen, and *Prison Games*[13] by Robert Ellis Heise alert us to the manipulation in a correction setting and provide suggestions for responding to it.

Since we have considered the types of facilities and a profile of the incarcerated, you might want to explore what your local jails are like and to check out the ministry needs of the inmates.

5

Getting Started in Detention Ministry

Taking the First Steps

As you consider getting involved in detention ministry, the ideal would be to find a facility with a chaplain who could help you get started. If you are interested in working at a local jail and there is no chaplain, you could call the chaplain at the closest state or federal facility for ideas and support. You might also inquire at the chancery office to see if anyone coordinates detention ministry in your diocese. A training program may even be in place. Or possibly your local St. Vincent de Paul Society Conference has resources or could find them for you.

The American Catholic Corrections Chaplains Association has national and regional meetings and resources to help with ministry to the incarcerated. The National Convocation of Jail and Prison Ministers also meets annually to provide programs and support for individuals ministering to prisoners (see p. 70 for address list). The ACCCA officers are listed on pp. 68–69 and can be contacted to find members who have volunteers in detention ministry.

Even if you are in a small town or parish, you may want to find someone else interested in detention ministry to work with you. The support would be invaluable, and doing things as a "team" enhances programming and other areas of the ministry.

The adults and youths that we meet in an incarcerated setting are persons like ourselves with feelings, values, questions, strengths, and areas of vulnerability. We have probably had support in times of joy and struggle to provide security and continuity for us. However, for the incarcerated, their lifestyle has been interrupted and fragmented and needs healing and understanding. It will take some experience to be truly helpful in this setting; feedback is an important aspect of this experience.

Institutional Rules

The following general rules are a helpful checklist for a volunteer minister to the incarcerated:

1. The volunteer must realize that SECURITY IS HIGHLY IMPORTANT IN ALL INSTITUTIONS. The job of the staff in detention facilities is to keep prisoners locked up. Detention ministers are "guests" who try to help inmates cope with their situation and provide them access to religious services.

2. The volunteer needs to determine what clearance procedures are expected before entering the facility. This will probably involve getting reference checks, a security clearance, fingerprinting, and obtaining a photo badge identification. The badge is the property of the institution and is to be returned when leaving the ministry. In many instances the badge can be pulled for breaking institutional rules.

3. The volunteer should get a clear list of "the do's and don'ts" for the facility he or she will enter.

4. Deputies and counselors must always be supported in the presence of the incarcerated, who will at times criticize the system. Volunteers do not have the background to understand the staff's problems or strategies. Therefore, while accepting the feelings of the incarcerated, volunteers should be supportive of the staff person's role. Great harm can be done by a

volunteer who fails to support the staff or who publicly rejects its authority.

5. Rules and regulations of each institution must always be supported. Volunteers should discuss questions with the administrators or with the coordinator of detention ministry. While conditions in the facilities are usually extreme, the volunteer may not always be aware of staff or budget constraints. If, however, a volunteer finds a pattern of activity unfair, he or she should discuss it with an administrator of the facility rather than "confront" a staff person.

6. No matter concerning the institution is to be discussed for publication in print or on television without the permission of the administrator of the institution.

7. Volunteers must realize that *consistency* in their service is essential and must be honored. In an emergency, arrangements should be made for substitutes and/or the institution and inmates should be notified.

8. Volunteers should not give their home address or telephone number to anyone incarcerated. One suggestion for communicating by mail is to arrange with a nearby pastor to have mail from an inmate sent to the parish house.

9. Nothing may be given to incarcerated persons without clearance from the administrator of the institution involved. The best policy is NEVER TO BRING ANYTHING INTO OR OUT OF THE INSTITUTION. The implication of contraband is always a serious issue. With longer sentences and the seriousness of offenses, the incarcerated can get very clever in creating mischievous as well as dangerous objects and weapons. Cigarettes or matches may never be given to youths. Gum, candy, pencils, and pens can be considered contraband. Ongoing permission may be received to distribute religious materials and articles.

10. Personal items (e.g., purses) should not be brought into a jail or prison. When umbrellas are taken into a facility, they must be left in the staff control area.

11. A volunteer may never pass notes or other forms of communication from one person to another without the permission of the staff. Any unusual movement of the persons during a session must be cleared with a deputy or counselor.

12. Persons doing programming in the facility must be aware of and conform to the schedules within the individual institution.

The REASONS for some of the above instructions may not be readily apparent. The instructions do, however, minimize dangers to the incarcerated themselves, as well as to the staff and others, from suicide, homicide, and other destructive behaviors.

Practical Points

While a volunteer will learn a lot by experience and local custom, a chart of the arrest process follows and a glossary of terms used in the criminal courts system is found on pp. 36–37. These are tools of reference for understanding what process the inmates have been through. Unless a person has been arrested, he or she cannot know what an inmate has experienced. Knowing some of the vocabulary can help with the dialogue.

Confidentiality

The chaplains and volunteers provide spiritual support and guidance and should obtain appropriate ecclesial Church authorization to minister in this regard.

Great care should be used to *never divulge private information* regarding the incarcerated or their families under any circumstances. Personal privacy and confidentiality are paramount in establishing trust and in maintaining a personal relationship. While newspaper reports make the alleged crimes "public information," the volunteer is frequently in a good position to see the facts or the situations differently and often gets quizzed on the sensational aspects of a case.

Within the facility, the incarcerated can be very clever about finding out information or sending messages to other inmates. One might suggest to them that they use the appropriate channels to communicate.

Most incarcerated persons have lived with lack of trust and broken promises in life. We need to change this in order to develop a sense of trust. This is one reason why many chaplains prefer to be paid by Church sources rather than give the impression that they are "part of the system" that has tended to oppress the incarcerated. Once lost, this trust is almost impossible to regain and neither our ministry nor our credibility will ever be as valued as before.

Sensitivity Toward Detention Staff

It will not take you long to become aware of the stress upon staff in a detention setting. It is not like a television program or movie. The facilities are overcrowded and usually understaffed. Budgets do not expand to the same degree that the population increases.

While we come and go throughout a facility, the staff usually spends an entire shift at a given post and does not have the option to leave when inmates' personalities are difficult.

We should be especially sensitive toward staff and their situations; time spent with them is time well spent.

It will take time for staff to understand our purpose and to feel comfortable with our movement throughout the facility. We can ask questions as we go but will probably do best by touring the facility and learning the rules before we go in for ministry.

Approaching a Person in Jail or Prison

As you probably suspect, one of the biggest challenges for the incarcerated is BOREDOM. Prisons usually have more programming than jails. Those in jail spend considerable time waiting: waiting to go to court, waiting for a lawyer, waiting for the next thing to happen. In many jails they cannot see outside, do not know the time of day and must cope with a world of noise, overcrowding and confusion.

At the very *least*, your visit will be a welcome distraction. Once you are identified as a chaplain, the inmates might "check you out" to see if you are a "do gooder" or they might try to determine what you are trying to get out of the experience. A great deal of the prisoners' style of relating to you will depend on their experience (or lack of experience) of God, Church and ministry. Most of their previous relationships have been built on using others and being used. Do not be surprised if they try some of this manipulation on you. Many prisoners have a close relationship with God and continue to process this during their time in jail. They will truly value your sharing this spiritual journey with them.

The important task is to establish a relationship in a caring way and then to listen patiently. When initiating a relationship, the volunteer should have an "agenda" to draw from that might be of interest—movies, sports, local happenings. It is *not appropriate* to ask why the inmate is in jail and expect an account of the offense. If this information is offered, it may be summarized but not dwelt upon. In the first place, the inmate has told the story so many times in and out of court that the account of the alleged crime is probably minimized. Or if the story is being related in earshot of others, the inmate will perhaps embellish it.

One approach that works is to notice things about the inmate's person or cell or talents that seem important to him or her. As we come in from the outside their world seems so small, but to them the "little" things are very important. Within their limited sphere I see them groom and dress up for religious services. Their interests and personalities are reflected in their cells, in what they collect and how they arrange it. I comment if I find them happy, articulate, engrossed in a game, an unusual activity or sport, a book or a letter home. What they like to watch on T.V. can give an insight. They will comment on something I notice long after I have forgotten about it.

Pastoral Presence in a Detention Setting

Whatever the initial dialogue is about, it is important to listen for the other's interests, gifts, patterns of behavior and feelings. One of the most effective ways of gaining insight is listening to a person's story and having that person reflect on his or her feelings. "What were you feeling? What are you feeling now? What is it like to feel _____? What usually happens when you feel _____?" Some feelings that we frequently encounter in jail are anger, fear, guilt, denial, depression and mistrust.

Another powerful tool in ministering to prisoners is a quiet environment, suitable for privacy. When it is time to listen to their stories, we may want to take them to a private nook away from distractions and noise or to an attorney room where God may enter the conversation more fully.

If we spend much time in one-on-one situations with incarcerated individuals, we should be sure that we have a strong support system to help us keep in touch with our own feelings and to help reinforce our listening skills. With all of the intensity of the correction setting, it is important that the volunteer keep centered and focused so as not to feed into manipulation or to control issues. Ongoing communication with someone who understands will help the volunteer to keep perspective and avoid burnout in order to maintain personal well-being and effectiveness in the ministry.

The qualities you will want to develop according to your own personality are those of honesty, caring and always being genuine. Being genuine is strategically important to this ministry. People who are incarcerated are finely tuned; their antennas are sensitive to any phoniness or disinterest on our part. Participating in this ministry gives one clearer insights into one's own life and feelings. Appropriately sharing one's own vulnerability and/or connectedness with Our Lord can be used as a model for the inmate or to establish more trust when needed.

The volunteer might reflect on the words of St. Paul, "Now not only I live, but Christ lives in me" (Gal. 2:20). As an instrument of Jesus Christ, much of the volunteer's time should be spent studying the techniques of Our Lord in relating to people, especially people with problems: the woman at the well (John 4:4-43) who responded to Jesus' thirst and so received his ministry, and the adulterous woman (John 8:53-9:12) and doubting Thomas (John 20:19-29) who showed vulnerability and yet were given the gift of peace. These are but a few of my favorite "Jesus with people" stories.

6

How Do I Know If It's for Me?

One morning in my office, I received a call from Mrs. Mary Clare Bennett, the mother of two teenagers in St. Cecilia's parish, who inquired, "How do I know if I have a call to detention ministry?" Mary Clare had attended a meeting in her parish on "How to Listen to Inmates." From the presentation and her dialogue with the chaplains and volunteers there, she could see that the needs were obvious, but what did she have to offer? Could someone other than a nun, a brother or a priest do any good? For a month she had kept the application papers hidden away, but something inside kept nagging at her to explore the possibilities.

When we met, I suggested that she consider the following questions and areas while gaining insight into the call to visit the imprisoned. I suggest that the reader take time to answer the initial question personally; then read the elaboration of the question and reflect on it again.

1. What type of relationship with God do I have?

Please note that this is not asking whether I am a good Catholic, whether I go to church on Sunday or how well I know my religion. Each of these aspects could be a part of the answer but questions more related to detention ministry would be:

a) Do I see God solely as my Judge? Is God a Savior who died on the cross to save me? What is God like?

b) Do I see myself as created in the image and likeness of God, developing my uniqueness and being challenged by my weaknesses and vulnerability?

c) Do I relate to God as a friend? How do I do this? If I don't, why not?

d) How do I deal with periods of dryness, challenges, and questions in my spiritual journey?

e) What helps to nurture my relationship with God?

In correction settings there is clearly an overall respect for God and religion. Even those who might not connect with religion at the time are generally sensitive to those who wish to respond to what the chaplaincy program offers. This is generally true of staff and inmates.

The time of incarceration can be a valuable time for many incarcerated persons to look at their lives, their values and frequently their spiritual journeys. The more we are in tune with our own spirituality, the more effective we will be in walking with the incarcerated in theirs. Br. John Baptist De La Salle, a teacher of pastoral ministry to the Christian Brothers, suggests that unless we pray, we will not "touch the hearts."[14] He also reminds us that "we cannot spread happiness around us by wearing a countenance like a prison door."[15]

2. How do I envision the role of a chaplain or volunteer?

The chaplaincy program includes pastoral counseling, religious services, religious programs (e.g. Bible studies), ecumenical programs, advocacy endeavors, and one-on-one visiting. These involve inmates, administration, staff, and relatives and friends of the incarcerated. In relation to this I might ask myself:

a) Do I think a volunteer needs to try to convert all of the inmates to Catholicism?

b) Do I see the volunteer as having or needing to have all of the answers to questions about the Catholic Church, the Bible, morality, social teaching and spirituality?

c) Would I find it necessary to try to respond to all of the spiritual needs of the incarcerated?

While the chaplain or volunteer would encourage any interest in the Catholic Church, the role of the detention ministry is not to proselytize but to relate to the unique spiritual journey of each inmate. If an inmate requests a chaplain of another faith, we try to respond.

A chaplain or volunteer who works in a detention setting will be asked many questions about the Catholic religion. It will be more important to look for appropriate resources for responses than to have the "answers" on hand or guess at them. I say "appropriate" resources because our responses must be clearly pastoral and not just simplistic or black and white "answers." One example of oversimplicity would be to suggest the Sacrament of Reconciliation as a total solution to an inmate's problems. If this sacred sacrament is not a part of the entire reconciliation process, it can be looked upon as a magical solution, a way of "conning" God, or bargaining with him rather than working on a relationship with him. The necessary steps to this relationship are hope, trust, forgiveness, conversion and love. An excellent book to help with this reconciliation process is Father Richard Gula's book *To Walk Together Again.*[16]

With the multiple aspects of detention ministry and the variety of personalities and needs of the incarcerated, it is helpful for the chaplain or volunteer to encourage others to join him or her. If you are just beginning a ministry or are interested in expanding the ministry in a given facility, it would be well worth your while to contact places where team ministry is already very effective. In addition to the enhancement of the ministry, the benefits of support and enhancement of the individual ministers are highly significant.

3. Do I have a sense of myself? Am I comfortable with myself?

Each of us is "in process" in these rapidly changing and challenging times, but it would be helpful to reflect:

a) Am I aware of my talents and gifts? How do I develop them?

b) Am I in touch with my weaknesses, limitations, vulnerabilities?

c) Am I comfortable with my sexuality and with sexual issues?

d) Do I have a clear support system?

e) How do I handle stress?

While for ordinary living it is helpful and productive to develop our strengths and talents, to be in touch with this when sharing with inmates can have powerful impact. It is *essential* that we are *genuine* about whatever we do in a correction setting and not put on airs or "mask" who we are. Inmates have lived with masks and walls and can see them for what they are. On the other hand, modelling any ways in which we are owning our own power and responding to God's unique plan for us will truly give a Christian witness.

Appropriately identifying and perhaps sharing our vulnerabilities and how we respond to our weaknesses, addictions and limitations will clearly demonstrate how we identify with the incarcerated in the need to respond to being saved. We reflect with the individual on the transcendence of God and the dignity and value of each person. Sharing how we personally deal with issues of anxiety, guilt, inferiority, and depression, or encouraging shared dialogue with the inmates can be an inspiration and a great lesson in self-acceptance. We find peace and joy in our realization of the unconditional love of God.

Many inmates have not had *any* appropriate relationships in their lives, let alone appropriate sexual relationships. The year I spent in chaplaincy training in a sex offender program truly helped me to value aspects of my personal life that I had taken for granted. A supportive home, a close relationship with my father, many friends of both sexes, and close professional relationships all helped me to learn—mostly by experience—the qualities of mutuality, respect, and care. The inmates in the sex offender program and many others incarcerated had not had these experiences. Their backgrounds included stories of child abuse, manipulation, addiction, and deprivation. Given their backgrounds and the fact that inmates are deprived of appropriate sexual activity while incarcerated, they can be vulnerable in relationships and attempt manipulative relationships.

For this very reason, I encourage appropriately feminine and appropriately masculine dress and decorum in a correction facility. The gifts that are peculiar to womanhood-manhood, sexuality and sensuality, can have a profound impact on pastoral relationships and liturgy and can assist one's spiritual journey. While having an appropriate relationship with a chaplain or volunteer of the same sex is valuable, the added dimensions of an *appropriate* relationship with the opposite sex can be profound. It can help the inmate get in touch with his or her own sexuality and it can model future relationships of any kind with the opposite sex. In order for this to happen, the chaplain or volunteer needs to *honestly* consider his or her own experiences of security in relationships with the opposite sex, be in touch with sexual feelings, and be prepared for the challenges of ministry in this setting.

Because of the vulnerability of the incarcerated, the intensity of this ministry, and the need for spiritual growth through it, a strong personal and pastoral support system is essential. This is a ministry calling for patience, adaptability, and the ability to cope with the stresses of the corrections system and the issues of the incarcerated. The chaplain or volunteer is frequently in the middle of issues that lie between the incarcerated and "the system." Because of confidentiality within the facility and on the outside, the chaplaincy role is unique and one frequently feels like no one understands. Being the voice of the voiceless is a challenge; the chaplain or volunteer is in the unique position of modelling Jesus' approach to the poor, the suffering, and the oppressed, and this today—as in Jesus' day—is not always a popular position. It is not necessarily a popular ministry even within the Church. In general, the public wants punishment, frequently without rehabilitation, unaware of the overwhelming complexity of the political, economic and sociological problems which have brought us to the inhumanness we see in the criminal justice system. With the rate of recidivism (persons with previous arrests returning to jail), we frequently feel no success with our endeavors.

Obviously, an adequate support system is needed to keep perspective in the face of all these issues, to avoid burnout and to continue to develop one's own spiritual, emotional, and personal resources for continued enrichment in this ministry.

The chaplain or volunteer will be working in a system where feelings, emotions, physical energy, and pressures are extremely intense.

Rev. Michael Bryant, a corrections chaplain at the jail in Washington, D.C., has training programs for detention ministers. He suggests that the chaplain or volunteer "needs to be integrated in his or her own personal life. A deep faith in God and in the sisters and brothers whom they serve must be the root of a chaplain's ministry. A seriously troubled person, in the difficult setting of the prison, would only bring added misery to self and to those served."[17]

In this regard, it is important that an individual going through a long period of extreme stress not commit to ministry inside the detention facility. During short term stressful periods—imminent death of a loved one, depression, severe illness, etc.—it would be best to get a temporary replacement. Correction system officials suggest that someone who has been

Felonies

ALLEGED CRIMINAL ACT Felonies	ARREST Retention in jail or release on bail or on own recognizance	CRIMINAL COMPLAINT Filed by district or county attorney's office if evidence warrants it	INITIAL APPEARANCE In district court without unnecessary delay. Informed of rights legal counsel assured	PRE H In d wit Pro: mus pro

Misdemeanor

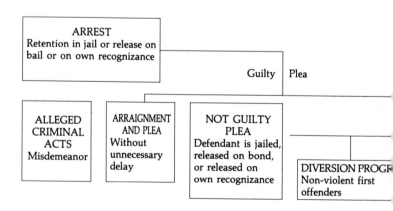

ARREST
Retention in jail or release on bail or on own recognizance

Guilty | Plea

ALLEGED CRIMINAL ACTS Misdemeanor	ARRAIGNMENT AND PLEA Without unnecessary delay	NOT GUILTY PLEA Defendant is jailed, released on bond, or released on own recognizance	
			DIVERSION PROGR Non-violent first offenders

ANNER, HOW AN ALLEGED OFFENDER
IINAL JUSTICE SYSTEM.

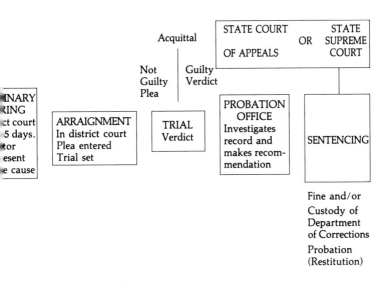

Acquittal

STATE COURT
OF APPEALS   OR   STATE SUPREME COURT

Not Guilty Plea

Guilty Verdict

INARY
RING
ct court
5 days.
tor
esent
e cause

ARRAIGNMENT
In district court
Plea entered
Trial set

TRIAL
Verdict

PROBATION
OFFICE
Investigates
record and
makes recom-
mendation

SENTENCING

Fine and/or
Custody of
Department
of Corrections
Probation
(Restitution)

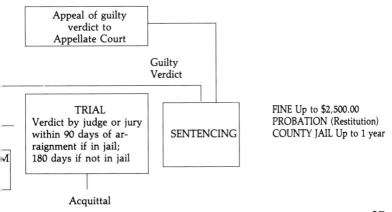

Appeal of guilty
verdict to
Appellate Court

Guilty
Verdict

TRIAL
Verdict by judge or jury
within 90 days of ar-
raignment if in jail;
180 days if not in jail

SENTENCING

FINE Up to $2,500.00
PROBATION (Restitution)
COUNTY JAIL Up to 1 year

Acquittal

addicted to alcohol or drugs have at least a year of recovery before getting involved in volunteer programs.

This is not to say that any of us always "have it all together," but it is strategic to this ministry to recognize the signs when we are in need of rest and relaxation.

On the other hand, those of us who *have* recognized and dealt with issues of anger, depression, addiction, or severe stress in our own lives and in relationships with others will be in a much better position to enable others to work through their problems. Again, by "others" we mean inmates, their families and friends, and all related to the criminal justice system. In our pain-filled world, some have become so turned in on themselves that they are hardly able to experience life at all.

4. *How do I see myself witnessing to gospel values?*

Can I witness to the Gospel in a way that is convincing and not obnoxious to people whose lifestyles often *seem* in contradiction to gospel values?

The Catholic volunteer might reflect on which gospel values were most in evidence in the Old and New Testaments and how these are challenged in our time. Prisoners are mentioned 125 times in the Bible and there are many specific examples of the imprisonment of heroes and saints in the Old Testament (Joseph, Samson, Psalmists, Isaiah and Jeremiah) and the New Testament (Jesus, John the Baptist, Peter and Paul). While these are sometimes helpful in observing how individuals related to issues involving incarceration, they provide insights into how gospel values can help us reach our potential according to God's unique plan for each of us.

I personally find the Old Testament themes of valuing creation, patience, and commitment most relevant to the corrections setting. As I indicated at the beginning of this booklet, I am clearly aware each time I go to jail or prison that it is by choice. This has led me to value my freedom, my privacy, and my potential to really appreciate all aspects of God's creation. Even in the restricted environment of the jail, many incarcerated sincerely try to use their time to see themselves as unique individuals, able to develop their talents and to use the gifts of creation to help them reach their potential.

As a chaplain in a correction facility, I sometimes say I'd be rich if I had a penny for every minute I wait: wait at the gates, wait for program and facility schedules, wait in the courtrooms, the attorney rooms and sometimes even to leave the facility. Yet all of this is minimal in comparison to the 24-hour a day wait that the incarcerated experience. Boredom, lack of privacy, and the oppression of the system make us easily able to identify with the patience of Job and other Old Testament persons and groups as they waited for signs of hope in the midst of tribulation.

The commitment of the volunteer to get and stay involved in this ministry is challenging given the initial preparation for getting started, the conditions of the facility and the system, and the fact that we rarely see the "results" of our efforts. For the inmate, commitment to continue on life's journey, given the reason for incarceration, the dehumanizing condition of incarceration, and the challenges facing the inmate upon release makes the psalms and the messages of Moses and the Old Testament prophets very real.

The New Testament is obviously rich with gospel values for this ministry. Jesus showed us how to pray, how to live and how to relate to others with compassion, honesty, and respect. Within the correction facility, the most difficult challenge is loss of control over one's own life and the struggle to have a self-image as a reasonably decent person. Many inmates have never experienced respect, let alone the unconditional love of God. The volunteer can be present to the inmate by accepting the real person, helping him or her see the good within, and understanding the struggles with hurts and insecurities. Religious volunteers have the great opportunity to bring the compassion of Jesus experienced in their own lives to touch others, to bond, to heal. The gospel values are shared in their very personhood—reaching out in hope and peace and joy as they journey with the inmate.

5. How do I relate to others?

It would be helpful for me to consider which age, sex, or personality type I feel most comfortable with and which gives me the most challenge. I might consider whether I prefer large group (e.g. leading religious services or bible studies), small group (e.g. rap sessions) or individual experiences (e.g. one-on-one visiting) and whether these would be formal or informal, structured or spontaneous. There is such a variety of people in jail that knowing one's preferences would be helpful in setting expectations.

7

Ministry Inside the Walls

Jails and local juvenile facilities offer the opportunity to be with adults or youths as they are newly arrested, awaiting trial, or serving shorter sentences. The ministry in these facilities is usually more directed toward helping people cope with initial incarceration and the unknown sentence. Volunteers provide religious services and individual support during this vulnerable time. Ongoing programming is a challenge, but the human spiritual need is obvious. The intensity and activity might be compared with the emergency room in a hospital. The developing of a sense of community or of long term relationships is clearly a challenge—given the nature of the facilities and the transient activity of the inmates, though the need is considerable.

Persons sentenced for longer periods are usually placed in camps or state facilities. Such individuals do not experience the fear and confusion of the unknown sentence and they are more interested in settling in and making the most of the extent of their stay. More in-depth pastoral counseling and religious programs prove very effective in this setting.

Relational Skills

Let's touch on some relational skills that are integral to detention ministry. We might ask ourselves which of these we come

by naturally through life experiences and which ones need fur-
ther development. If we are in touch with how we relate to
others, our experience in a detention setting will alert us to areas
we want to develop.

Caring is the heartbeat of any volunteer program. Inmates
are truly impressed that persons are willing to freely and
genuinely share in their lives. The Catholic volunteer offers
something that no other agency, resource, or program provides. To quote an inmate from San Quentin, "Volunteers add
relevance to the chapel situation . . . [they] are perceived to
be people that are genuinely interested in the well-being of the
inmates. After all, they are not paid. With correct personal
motives, the volunteers are essential to adding 'The Human
Touch.'"

Acquainting oneself with the facility by going with others,
observing other programs or at least touring the facility can
help the volunteer feel more at ease. Some volunteers are in-
timidated at first by guards (in prisons), deputies (in jails),
and/or inmates. It helps to think of each of these groups as
people like ourselves.

An occasional guard will not understand the role of the religious volunteer and will project the attitude that you are a
detriment to security for which the guard is responsible. Even
when programs and visits are prearranged and cleared, the staff
might express concern that these volunteers are bleeding
hearts—innocent, naive, warmhearted—victims for the con
artist.

The prisoners will wonder if the volunteer is there on his
or her own or as part of "the system." Since most have lived
lives of broken promises and relationships, it will take a long
time to develop trust. Being a religious volunteer sometimes
helps, but it is still up to the individual to establish a personal
style of communicating in this setting.

Experience will give the volunteer more objectivity in working with inmates and staff and in trying to see the impact of

the role on the person. While some staff overreact to volunteers, security *is* their main concern. As caring persons we will have feelings of sadness, concern, and joy which we will learn to keep in perspective as we experience the various layers of manipulation of staff and prisoners. I find that the caring becomes reciprocal with both staff and inmates. For the inmates, we are frequently their only significant contact with the outside world and they value sharing in our interests and concerns. I am frequently aware of their sensitivity and am touched by their simple thoughtfulness on my behalf.

The Ministry Program

Communication concerns can sometimes be alleviated by clarifying the volunteer's expectations of administration, staff, inmates, and self. If your diocese or parish already has a program, the administration has probably already approved the program and the clearance procedures. If you wish to start a detention ministry program, you might want to contact existing programs and modify their ideas to your needs. A few of the dioceses with existing programs in the United States and Canada are listed on p. 72. Another suggestion, in this case, would be to contact the administrator and see what programs currently exist and what are the perceived needs. Depending on one's time, interest, and resources, a program could be developed and reviewed by the administrator. Having the backing and support of others in the Church community would be strategic to this process. It is always best to start simply, get established, and expand as needed.

With staff, it is important to inform them as needed of a personal program for involvement as a volunteer. If a program is already developed, it probably includes an orientation to the facility and existing programs. One should also be clear about the particular procedures for each facility. Until volunteers feel comfortable with their role of pastoral presence and develop a rapport with inmates, they might tend to compare their role with those of other staff—probation officers, deputies, medical staff, program staff, etc.—and feel inadequate as the others are all clearly "doing something" whereas the results of religious presence is not quite so obvious.

Don't worry if you don't connect with inmates right away. It takes time (if it ever happens) to get used to jail or prison. Until you share the inmates' stories and relate to them, they will probably just be curious about your presence. Once they know what you are about, they will express their appreciation in various ways. Some volunteers want to speed up the process so they start bringing things to the inmates like Rosaries, holy cards, books, etc. Religious articles *do* have a place, but should be used in response to a need of the inmate, rather than of a perceived need on the part of the volunteer. Some facilities will not permit these because the inmates wear them as jewelry (even designer jewelry!) or trade them for contraband or drugs. Inmates can then start to use the volunteer to bring in other commissary items and books and do other errands. The simplest thing is to establish clear limits from the very beginning (obviously keeping within the rules of the facility). The best rule of thumb is usually to bring in nothing. This is easiest to establish and gets the inmate to focus on your being there because you care rather than manipulating you. It is best to be fair and firm and not to hedge. The prisoners will appreciate it more and you'll find you'll wonder where the time has gone—the needs are so great. . . .

In developing good communication with inmates, the religious volunteer will want to consider the following points:

1. *Never diminish anyone's human dignity.*

   a. Make the other person right in something (something genuine).
   b. Avoid finding fault.

    c. Avoid arguments.

    d. Admit your own mistakes.

2. *Develop an honest interest in other people.*

    a. Be an interested listener.

    b. Become sincerely concerned about the needs, desires, and interests of others.

3. *Recognize individual uniqueness and worth.*

    a. Try to get names correctly and use them often.

    b. Be appreciative and quick to give approval.

    c. Don't take desired behavior for granted and remember to show appreciation of it.

    d. Respect the rights and opinions of others.

4. *Cooperate with the wants of other people.*

    a. Encourage initiation.

    b. Help the other person get what is best for them by helping themselves.

    c. Present problems and ask solutions.

    d. Present doubts, opinions, or objections in question form, asking "How" questions instead of "Why" questions.

Having self-expectations is important. It won't take you long to find that you receive more than you give. Just be yourself and do what you are about. Your spiritual life will deepen as you pray for the guidance of the Spirit working through your unique healing presence in the correction facility. Keep developing the strengths of listening and relating. Avoid the weaknesses of becoming immune to the system or burning out by not setting clear limits and not having a clear support system. A sense of humor will probably be your biggest asset. Try not to take yourself too seriously. Let go and let God.

Survey Results on Religious Volunteers in a Correction Setting

In preparation for this pamphlet, I polled prison and jail staff, chaplains, volunteers, and inmates at San Quentin and received over 75 responses. Some ideas were included in the discernment process (chapter 6), but the following is a summary of the most frequent responses:

What three qualities would you see as most desirable in a religious volunteer in a correction setting?

I've organized the responses into four categories with the most frequent responses listed first:

• *Witness Gospel Values:* Faith, understanding, honesty, commitment, prayer, self-forgiving, patience, hope.

• *Compassion:* Non-judgmental, caring, enjoy people, loving, charitable, sense of humor.

• *Communication Skills:* Ability to listen (the most frequently mentioned = 34 times), self-expressing, insightful, tactful.

• *Common Sense:* Self-acceptance, tolerance, professionalism, wholistic approach, strength.

For persons trying to decide if "this is for them," what two questions might they ask themselves?

The most frequently suggested questions were:

1. Am I willing to be consistent?
2. Can I value prisoners as persons?
3. Am I responding to God's call—willing to find Jesus in this work?
4. Do I believe ministry is possible in this environment?
5. Can I stay vital in the enervating and depressing atmosphere of the jail?

Probably the biggest problem for religious volunteers in a correction setting is:

1. manipulation by staff, the system, and inmates.
2. unrealistic expectations.
3. working with the reality of the system.
4. time for adequate preparation and support.
5. creatively adapting to the depressing atmosphere.

What advice would you give to volunteers just starting out?

1. Be ready for the unexpected—prepared but flexible.
2. Take your time, develop trust (communicate with everyone possible to get all the perspectives on institutional life).
3. Provide a variety of dimensions of normal lives and normal relationships.
4. Appreciate the charisms enjoyed by a strong lay apostolate.
5. Respond to a broader variety of ministries within the facility.
6. Respond to cultural diversity.

In general, prisoners do not trust themselves to be authentic, so they wear masks and act out roles. Many are suffering from anxiety, guilt complexes, or inferiority complexes. Since one's image of self is the motivating factor for most behavior, the volunteer should take the time to enable his or her own goodness, beauty, and potential to show. Hopefully, the inmate can begin to feel less need for the masks and make more appropriate choices toward personal growth. This journey can be spiritually enriching for the volunteer as well as the inmate.

8

Other Volunteer Experiences Inside

While the focus of the religious volunteer is clearly spiritual, other areas of volunteerism within the facility can provide a source of contact with "people who care."

Volunteers with other skills offer their services in organizing and distributing library books, tutoring (reading, G.E.D., etc.) or teaching art, music, sports, crafts, drama, aerobics, and physical fitness. Other services are offered by beauticians, barbers, and individuals able to organize entertainment or refreshments for holidays and special occasions.

Volunteers can be trained in procedures for appropriately responding to inmate needs—contact with family, attorneys, employers. Others help the inmates with bail, courtroom issues and pre-release orientation.

Some volunteers visit individual inmates for ongoing support. Two programs that are well organized for matching individuals and inmates and helping with this process are the Match Two (M-2) Program at San Quentin (M-2 Sponsors, Inc., San Quentin, CA 94964) and the Service League in San Mateo County, California, program for jails (878 Main St., Redwood City, CA 94063).

Since most incarcerated are in prison or jail because of issues of addiction (e.g., alcohol or drug related issues), support groups such as Alcoholics Anonymous, Narcotics Anonymous, Sex Anonymous, Overeaters Anonymous, etc., provide sessions according to need. There are now support groups for women interested in getting out of prostitution, such as Women Emerging, where ex-prostitutes and group facilitators work with the inmates. Going in with a support group might be a way for a volunteer interested in religious services to get started and then expand according to need. It is suggested that all volunteers attend at least one meeting of some group which deals with addiction. The programs work for many people and the techniques used could be transferred to other areas of ministry.

Two programs that use volunteers inside the facility and out are God Accepting the Exiled (GATE) and Victim Offender Reconciliation Programs (VORP). GATE (3871 Piedmont Ave., Oakland, CA 94611) is an organization that provides specialized educational and support services to those who have been traditionally exiled from the mainstream of society, particularly the incarcerated.

The organization seeks to promote inner healing through classroom teaching, retreats, group and individual support, and the provision of educational materials. Specialized techniques using guided imagery (visualization of a desired effect) are taught for the purpose of increasing self-acceptance, promoting a greater sense of self-worth, and improving communication with self and others. Through the use of guided imagery exercises, meditations, drawing, and discussion, a person is instructed in how to access personal potential for inner healing.

The spiritual basis of the organization is the belief that the source of unconditional love and truth lives within each of us and that this love is the primary source of inner reconciliation, healing, and wholeness. Through relationship with this love, the inner exiled parts of ourselves are accepted, transformed, and set free.

Fr. Thomas Schubeck, S.J., in *Who Is the Prisoner?*, notes that "the value of Victim Offender Reconciliation Programs and Community Boards is threefold: they reduce and even eliminate hostility between conflicting parties; they promote the good of the community by restoring peace; and they satisfy the demands of justice. Their principles are thus related to the Gospel imperative to forgive one's enemies, as well as to the broader human demand for restitution."[18] Both programs have volunteer training guidelines for these ministries.

9

Detention Ministry Without Going to Jail

After visiting a corrections facility and/or discerning (considering) your involvement in this ministry, you might like to get involved—but not inside. You are probably convinced of the need for advocacy efforts for inmates, their families and victims of crime, but you do not feel that your life experiences have led you to deal with the intensity inside the jail or prison. There are several opportunities available:

Advisory Boards

The Detention Ministry Advisory Board of the Archdiocese of San Francisco recommends and sets guidelines with the detention ministry coordinator to carry out a program for this ministry. When they first began, they developed a philosophy, basic policies and resources for chaplains and volunteers. Membership on the board consists of representatives of persons involved in the criminal justice system, other resources for the incarcerated and their families, members of various culture groups, and residents of different geographical areas of the archdiocese. They continue to support and advise on issues and concerns in the expansion of the ministry to better meet the needs of the inmates. Other dioceses have similar boards, some of which are part of a broader program of advocacy and criminal justice. More information on boards can be obtained from the various dioceses published in the Resources on pp. 67–68. Volunteers who are interested in program development and issues or advisory board involvment might prefer this vital response to the spiritual needs of the incarcerated and advocacy issues on their behalf.

Inmate Services

Some of the larger county jail systems have Prisoner Services or Service League Organizations which depend on volunteers because of limited staff. Drop-in centers for inmates upon release and development of resources for post-release inmates are a couple of the services offered by these volunteers. There is also an organization, Friends Outside, that trains volunteers how to provide services for inmates on release from prison or jail.

Two programs for imprisoned women who have children are the Lamp Program, 1004 N. Elm St., Greensboro, N.C. 27401, and the Match Program, 247 Harris Road, Bedford Hills, NY 10507. Detention ministry in New York has excellent programs for inmates at each stage of incarceration.

Visiting Centers

A vital extension of ministry to inmates is concern for their families. Frequently the families suffer more—being on the outside and having to face the implications of the incarceration—than the inmate who is hidden away and enduring punishment with others "in the same boat."

In 1971, Sr. Maureen Fenlon encouraged the development of a program of hospitality for families of inmates at San Quentin out of which The House was begun. The mission of The House is to promote prison visiting in order to maintain family ties during imprisonment and improve the inmates' chances for successful re-entry into society upon release. Volunteer jobs in this program include providing information and support concerning issues involved with visiting inside, van driver, kitchen workers, providing child care, maintaining connections with service resource centers, house maintenance, coordinating clothing distribution, fund raising, and many other hospitality and support services.

While The House started simply, it has now developed into a network of prison visitors' centers around the country. In Marin County, California, it is sponsored by Catholic Social Services and Centerforce. If a prison near you has a program in need of such services, you might be interested in offering yourself, or if they don't, you might want to send for the Volunteer Guide *The House at San Quentin*, c/o Catholic Social Service, San Quentin, CA 94964 for ideas to be adapted for your area.

Many jails also have visitor centers to support the visitors who are under tremendous strain, intensified by constant concern for the inmate. Volunteers provide child care while adults visit, arrange for supervised contact visits for the inmates with their children, and offer basic information and support for all involved in the visiting process.

Pen Pals

Many persons who are unable to become involved in direct ministry are interested in corresponding with someone incarcerated. This is usually more effective in a prison than in the transitory setting of a jail.

Sr. Alice Larson, S.H.F., coordinator of detention ministry in the diocese of Monterey,[19] has developed the following guidelines for persons interested in becoming pen pals:

Use a post office box number or the box number of a public location, i.e., work, an agency, or local church.

Keep any friendship which develops honest and realistic.

Since friendships are always a gradual process, hang onto your photos, even when asked, until you feel ready. Anxiety and loneliness hang heavy for the incarcerated and they may try to rush the friendship.

The pen pal system is synonymous with friendship, not evangelization, preaching, or counsel. Most inmates do not solicit religious advice until they are ready, and some never do ask.

Ask inmates about things they like to do and respond to other things they choose to share.

Be cautious if you share things about yourself and family; some inmates may use your remarks inappropriately. Sometimes on the outside we run into a person who is snoopy about our private lives or pumps for information, and occasionally we may meet an inmate with the same fault; if so, just refuse to answer. Your directness will be accepted by the inmate. It goes without saying that we do not need to ask the inmate why he or she has been incarcerated. The inmate is trying to put the best foot forward, to be liked, just like you. The present moment is important; the past is finished and the time for change and growth is in the present instant.

Sometimes exchanged letters begin to take on a romantic twist (like the mail order bride/groom concept). If dependency or "falling in love" starts to develop, it is essential to be clear in the expectations, even if it means terminating an exchange with this particular inmate.

If you are interested in sending something to the inmate, you might consider colorful photos of a beautiful place, a *few* stamps, greeting cards, bookmarks, articles on different subjects—but keep it simple.

Do not make promises you cannot keep. An inmate might write frequently (they have more time) and expect the same in return. Clarifying expectations and setting limits in all of these areas will help the inmate to understand appropriate mutuality in relationships.

These are general suggestions for penpals. If you are interested in this ministry, you might want to contact the Catholic chaplain at your closest state and federal prison for name(s). You might ask for any rules or suggestions regarding writing or sending anything to inmates at that facility. It might also be wise to stay in touch with the chaplain regarding how your correspondence is going.

Parish Involvement

Three types of parish involvement that may be encouraged are education, motivation, and concern for incarcerated inmates from one's parish.

Education: As indicated, the correction system is not working. Conditions are inhumane, and the United States criminal justice system is considered barbaric by other countries. Only the U.S.S.R. and South Africa have higher per capita numbers incarcerated than the U.S. does. Perhaps people involved in social justice issues could help with advocacy efforts for the incarcerated and be encouraged that their involvement in alleviating the social problems of the poor, the abused, and the addicted can be a preventative of incarceration.

Knowledge of what is happening or could be happening in detention ministry locally would be enriched by having a chaplain or religious volunteer speak to your parish or other group to learn firsthand about the conditions and the particular spiritual needs of the incarcerated in your area. The parish would see that frequently religious services are the only form of rehabilitation offered. Since the expansion of the ministry outside of state and federal prisons is relatively new except in larger cities, many parishioners are probably not even aware of how to respond to the gospel mandate "to visit the imprisoned" (Matt 25:36).

In addition to finding out the possibilities for involvement in the ministry, inviting a person involved in the ministry provides the parishioners who wish the opportunity to show support for this individual. Full time chaplains are also imprisoned (locked up) 40+ hours a week and responding continually to very intense situations. A possible involvement for your parish could be to adopt a correction chaplain and pray for the individual and the ministry. There is clearly a need for support to avoid burnout and frustration. I find my greatest source of personal strength is the knowledge that the sisters in our own infirmary and retirement center remember me in their daily prayers and sufferings.

Motivation: The prevailing trend is to be "tough on crime," "lock them up and throw away the keys," leading to an "out of sight, out of mind" mentality.

The Christian response is counter-cultural: "Remember those who are in prison as though you were in prison with them. Remember those who are suffering as though you were suffering as they are." (Heb. 13:3).

Winston Churchill once observed that the test of any society's level of civilization was the way it treated its poor, aged, children, handicapped, and, very importantly, its prisoners.

Practically speaking, prisoners have forfeited their freedom as a result of their acts, but we must be concerned about them as persons, unconditionally loved by God. Approximately 97 percent of all prisoners are released at some time. Warden Daniel Vasquez at San Quentin remarked that every day he takes inmates in and every day others are released back into communities and neighborhoods.

With the thousands of prisons and jails in operation today and the number of incarcerated steadily increasing, many volunteers are needed to help reduce the evil effects of prison life and provide for pastoral care.

Concerns for Incarcerated Inmates from Your Parish: One imperative that I would like to see our Church have is to overcome the opinion that the jail or prison is solely the responsibility of the parish where it is located. For sacramental reasons this is sometimes necessary, but inmates come from all parishes and the parish community should respond to the needs of both a community member while he or she is incarcerated and the prisoner's family (if appropriate), as well as offering support to pre-release and post-release programs and welcoming the individual back into the community upon release.

Like the volunteer who works inside the facility, the parishioner should not expect that incarceration will alter or change the personality of the prisoner or enable the building of a new one. Facing the real self is difficult for any of us, let alone a person who has been publicly labeled a criminal and thought by some to be unworthy of human society. Acceptance back into the community could be the strongest deterrence to recidivism.

Participation in support groups for ex-offenders would be one area of ministry. For some ex-inmates this would be sufficient, but others would need a more structured transitional program back into the community. The Archdioceses of Boston, Washington, D.C., and New York, as well as other dioceses and individuals and groups offer structured post-release programs for resident ex-offenders as well as community centers providing non-resident services to facilitate entrance back into the community.

When the Prisoners Union in San Francisco honored a dozen ex-offenders who had successfully made the transition back into society, they each mentioned the support of their families and others who were willing to believe in them as essential to their present positions in the area.

Conclusion

Prayer: In detention ministry we are asking the hard questions:

- Do I really believe in God's unconditional love?
- Do I really believe that God can change anyone?
- Do I really believe that God's grace is sufficient for all?

Whether I am able to volunteer directly in correction facilities or with other agencies outside the facility or indirectly by support and prayer for the ministry, my prayer should be faith-filled. Dr. Timothy McCarthy teaches that the three ingredients of faith are conviction, commitment and confidence.

My prayer will grow in the *conviction* (knowledge) that this ministry is a gospel mandate and my awareness and involvement *will* make a difference. "God expects us to perform good deeds" (Eph. 2:10).

My prayer will enhance my *commitment.* I will be filled with an awareness of God's total love, concern, and acceptance of me, of those inside. I will model how to love with no strings attached in spite of obstacles and manipulation.

My prayer will give me the *confidence,* the trust that I can journey with Christ the Prisoner in each person in the correction facility. This journey would reflect a God whose love is a gift freely given and freely received by those who desire it. It would engender a confidence in the forgiving God which would enable me to experience spiritual liberation.

Notes

1. J. L. Houlden, *Paul's Letters from Prison* (Baltimore: Penguin Press, 1970) 69.

2. Hugo Hoever, *Lives of the Saints* (New York: Catholic Book Publishing Company, 1977).

3. John Henry Abbott, *In the Belly of the Beast* (New York: Random House, 1944).

4. Jerry Graham, *Where Flies Don't Land* (Dallas: Acclaimed Books, 1977).

5. Dietrich Bonhoeffer, *Prayers From Prison* (Toronto: Griffin House, 1975).

6. Benjamin E. Chavis, *Psalms From Prison* (New York: Pilgrim Press, 1983).

7. Ambrosio Romero Cerranza, *The Vincentian Charism in the Laity—Frederick Ozanam* (Vincentian Studies Institute VII, no. 1, 1986) 89.

8. *Ibid.* 95.

9. Ron Atwood, *The American Penitentiary: An Experiment* (San Francisco: Humanity Productions, 1976).

10. United States Department of Justice Statistics Bulletin, October, 1987.

11. Stephen Michaud, *The Only Living Witness* (New York: Signet, 1983).

12. Bud Allen, *Games Criminals Play* (Susanville, California: Rae John Publ., 1981).

13. Robert Ellis Heise, *PRISON GAMES, Games Convicts Play, Staff Games, The Convict Code* (Fort Worth, Texas 76112, P.O. Box 8694, "Two in a Cell").

14. *Gleanings From the Life and Writings of Saint John Baptist de La Salle* (New York: La Salle Bureau) 41.

15. *Ibid.* 31.

16. Richard Gula, *To Walk Together Again* (New York: Paulist Press, 1984).

17. George Anderson, S.J. and others, *Who Is the Prisoner?* (New Orleans: Institute of Human Relations, 1985) 154.

18. Thomas Schubeck, S.J., "Reconciliatory Response to Crime," *Who Is the Prisoner?* (New Orleans: Institute of Human Relations, 1985) 63–69.

19. Sr. Alice Larson, *Some Thoughts for Pen Pals: Prison Ministry* (Diocese of Monterey, California).

Terms Used in the Criminal Court System

Police

AFFIDAVIT: written or printed declaration or statement of facts, made voluntarily, and confirmed by the oath or affirmation of the party making it, taken before an officer having authority to administer such an oath.

ARREST: the legal apprehension and restraint of a person suspected of a crime so that he may be brought to stand trial.

BOOKING: the process of finger-printing, photographing, and recording the arrest of a suspect at a police station.

CHARGE: the crime with which the person is accused.

COMPLAINT: in a criminal action, the person who brings the facts to the attention of the police authorities; the legal document filed by the district attorney charging the person with the commission of a crime.

CONTRABAND: any article the possession of which is illegal.

FELONY: a criminal act punishable by confinement in a state prison.

MISDEMEANOR: a criminal act punishable by confinement in a city or county jail for up to one year, by a fine, or both.

PROBABLE CAUSE: a state of facts as would lead a person of ordinary care and prudence to believe and conscientiously entertain an honest and strong suspicion that a person is guilty of a crime.

STATUTE: a law enacted by a legislature or law-making body.

WAIVER: the voluntary surrender of one's legal rights.

WARRANT: an order issued by a magistrate directing a law officer to carry out an arrest or search.

Courts

ACQUITTAL: the legal and formal certification of a finding of "not guilty" of a person who has been charged with a crime.

APPEAL: the review by a higher court of a trial held in a lower court on the complaint that an error has been committed.

ARRAIGNMENT: the part of the process in which the accused is called before the court, informed of the charge against the person, advised of his or her rights, and asked to enter a plea of "guilty" or "not guilty." The accused enters his or her plea, and it is recorded.

BAIL: the security given to the court in exchange for the release of a person in custody to assure his or her presence in the court.

CONFESSION: a statement made by a person charged with a crime in which that person acknowledge himself or herself to be guilty of the charge.

CONTEMPT: the disobedience of the rules, orders, or processes of the court.

CONVICTION: the result of a criminal trial that ends with a finding of guilt.

DEFENDANT: the accused in a criminal case.

DELIBERATION: the consideration given by the jury to a case so that it may arrive at its verdict.

EVIDENCE: any of the various types of information, including testimony documents, and physical objects that a court allows a lawyer to introduce in a legal proceeding in order to convince the court or the jury of the truth of his or her client's contention.

EX POST FACTO: legislation having retroactive effect to establish a crime or increase punishment or remove a defense to a crime.

GRAND JURY: a body of the required number of persons returned from the citizens of the county before a court of competent jurisdiction and sworn to inquire into public offenses committed or triable within the county.

HABEAS CORPUS: a writ or court order requiring that a prisoner be brought before a court to determine whether he or she is being legally held.

IMMUNITY: the protection given a witness against a criminal prosecution in return for information.

INDICTMENT: an accusation in writing presented by a grand jury to a competent court and charging a person with a public offense.

JUDGE: public officer who presides over and administers a court of law. The judge's principal responsibility is to insure that the trials held in the court are fair and equitable.

JURISDICTION: the legal authority which a court has to try a case.

JURY: a body of citizens who are selected to hear and decide a case; in a criminal court, twelve people serve on the jury.

MAGISTRATE: an officer or a judge having power to issue a warrant for the arrest of a person charged with a public offense or for the search of a designated place for contraband.

ORDER OF THE COURT: a formal direction requiring that a certain act be performed or restrained.

PARDON: an act of clemency by the governor of a state which restores to a convicted person some or all of his or her rights, privileges, and franchises of which he or she has been deprived in consequence of the conviction.

PAROLE: the conditional release of a prisoner before he or she has served his or her full sentence.

PERJURY: the willful giving of false evidence or testimony while under oath in a judicial proceeding on a material, or relevant, matter.

PLAINTIFF: the accusor in a criminal case, which is the government in the name of the people.

PLEA: an accused person's answer to a charge or indictment against him or her.

PLEA BARGAIN: a plea bargain is an agreement in a criminal case between the defense attorney and prosecuting attorney made with the consent of the judge and the defendant. In a plea bargain the defendant agrees to plead guilty to a crime that is less serious than the one charged rather than go to trial. The defense and prosecution may negotiate a mutually satisfactory disposition of the case. This allows a case to be completed quickly, and the judge then sentences the accused.

PRISON: the words "prison" and "penitentiary" are used synonymously to designate institutions for the imprisonment of persons convicted of more serious crimes. They are state-operated as distinguished from city and county jails.

PROBATION: a type of suspended sentence in criminal cases. A person on probation can go free, usually under the supervision of a probation officer, as long as he or she remains on good behavior.

PROBATION REPORTS: a written report prepared by a probation officer which contains the family history of the accused; his or her personal history including health, education and criminal background; evaluation of the crime and recommendations for restitution, for probation, or for institutionalization. The report is prepared for the judge as a guide in setting a proper sentence for the offender.

PROSECUTOR: the lawyer who conducts the government's case against a person accused of a crime.

RECIDIVIST: a person who reverts to criminal activity after conviction for a crime.

SENTENCE: the formal judgment in a criminal proceeding in which the judge states the penalty or punishment for a defendant who has been convicted of a crime.

SUBPOENA: a process issued out of court requiring a witness to attend a court hearing.

TESTIMONY: an oral statement of evidence given by a witness under oath.

TRANSCRIPT: an official written copy of the proceedings in a court.

VERDICT: the determination of the jury.

VOIR DIRE: a preliminary examination made by a court or attorney of one presented as a juror or witness in regard to his or her competency.

General

AKA: abbreviation for *also known as* or "alias"

BULLET: one-year sentence.

BUSTED: arrested

CAMP: a minimum security jail facility operated by the sheriff's office. Emphasis of the program is rehabilitation instead of punishment.

CAPITAL OFFENSE: (used in Bill of Rights), a crime punishable by death.

CONDITION OF PROBATION: the court frequently imposes conditions when it grants probation; generally, it has been held that

the conditions must be related to the offense, e.g., making restitution for damage done while committing an offense. The most
common special conditions are that the probationer report to the
probation officer and keep him or her informed as to employment
and residence and that he or she obey all laws.

CONTRABAND: (illegal); anything not authorized by jail to be
brought in to an inmate.

COURT APPEARANCE: a defendant's physical appearance in a court.

DETENTION: forcibly kept in custody, as a person may be "detained"
for forty-eight hours legally without being arraigned.

DISTRICT ATTORNEY: a county attorney responsible for the prosecution of criminals for crimes committed in that county.

GRASS OR POT: marijuana

INDICTMENT: a formal written accusation by a grand jury charging that a crime has been committed.

JOINT: a state institution; Department of Corrections.

MODIFICATION OR BEING MODIFIED: length of sentence reduced
by the court, e.g., conditions of probation accomplished by a peti-
tioning of the court usually by the probation officer. As an example, a changed set of circumstances, e.g., loss of job prevents
the probationer from fulfilling a condition of probation like a fine,
and the probation officer might then ask for deletion of deferment
of this condition through a "petition for modification."

(O.R.) (OWN RECOGNIZANCE): a release from custody without
posting bail on a promise to appear in court as ordered and following an interview and investigation of a person's relative sta-
bility.

PAROLE: the release from custody of a prisoner under the supervisor
of prison authorities. If the prisoner violates the terms of his or
her release, he or she is subject to return to prison to finish the
balance of the prison term. Criminal courts no longer have control over a prisoner after their commitment to prison; they remain
under the exclusive control of the paroling authority.

P.D. (PUBLIC DEFENDER, PRIVATE DEFENDER): Court appointed
attorney.

PLEA: "to make a plea," in a criminal case, is a statement in court
by the defendant, as to whether he or she pleads guilty or not guilty
or does not wish to contest the matter.

P.O. (PROBATION OFFICER): probation officer or parole officer.

PRE-SENTENCE REPORT: following the conviction of an offender for a felony, the court *must* refer the matter to the probation officer for the completion of a social study *and* a recommendation *for* or *against* granting probation; this is mandatory even in cases where the defendant apparently is ineligible for probation, as outlined in Section 1203 of the Penal Code. In cases of misdemeanors, the court may refer the matter to the probation officer for pre-sentence report. The defendant *does not* have to accept probation.

PRIORS: previous convictions may be charged. If they are prior convictions, such as those enumerated in Section 1203 of the Penal Code, they may render him or her technically ineligible for probation.

PROBATION: a period of time specified in an order signed by the judge during which the convicted person can be at liberty, subject to supervision by the probation department. Violation of probation requirements can bring about a jail term. Sometimes the judge makes a stay in jail a condition of probation.

PROSECUTE: attempting to prove that a defendant or defendants committed a crime or crimes. The district attorney's office, representing the people, prosecutes.

PUBLIC DEFENDER: a court appointed attorney responsible for the defense of criminals charged with crimes in that county who cannot afford to hire their own attorney.

RESTITUTION: reimbursement to the victim of a crime for a loss or expenses incurred because of the crime. Often imposed as a condition of probation.

REVOCATION OF PROBATION: a court action to terminate a grant of probation and to impose the heretofore suspended sentence. The action may be initiated by the probation officer, the district attorney's office, or the court for a variety of reasons but usually because of a new crime.

STATE PRISON: a state facility where convicted felons serve their sentence.

STATUTE: a rule of law passed by a legislative body, usually the state legislature or Congress, as opposed to an ordinance, passed by city councils and boards of supervisors.

TIME SERVED: time in jail served.

Bibliography

Abbott, Jack Henry. *In the Belly of the Beast.* Vintage Books, 1981.
Allen, Bud, and Pasta, Diana. *Games Criminals Play.* Susanville, Calif.: Rae John Publishers, 1981.
Anderson, George, et al. *Who Is the Prisoner?* New Orleans: Institute of Human Relations, 1985.
Bonhoeffer, Dietrich. *Prayers From Prison.* Philadelphia: Fortress Press, 1965.
Buckley, Marie. *Breaking into Prison.* Boston: Beacon Press, 1974.
DeWolf, L. Harold. *What Americans Should Do About Crime.* San Francisco: Harper & Row, 1976.
Ellis, Albert and Harper, Robert. *A New Guide to Rational Living.* North Hollywood: Wilshire Book Company, 1975.
Gula, Richard. *To Walk Together Again.* Ramsey, N.J.: Paulist Press, 1984.
Hart, Thomas. *The Art of Christian Listening.* New York: Paulist Press, 1980.
Jackson, Bruce. *Killing Time: Life in the Arkansas Penitentiary.* Ithaca, N.Y.: Cornell University Press, 1977.
Michaud, Stephen and Agnesworth, Hugh. *The Only Living Witness.* New York: Linden Press, 1983.
Nouwen, Henri. *The Wounded Healer.* New York: Wonder Books, 1979.
Peck, M. Scott. *People of the Lie.* New York: Simon and Schuster, 1983.
Sanford, John. *Evil, The Shadow Side of Reality.* New York: Crossroad Publishers, 1981.

Smedes, Lewis B. *Forgive and Forget; Healing the Hurts We Don't Deserve.* San Francisco: Harper and Row, 1984.

Sonkin, Daniel. *Learning to Live Without Violence.* San Francisco: Volcano Press, 1982.

Resources

1) Diocesan Coordinators:

Sr. Betty Bender
Archdiocese of Portland, Oregon
2838 Burnside St.
Portland, OR 97214

Rev. Michael Bryant
Coordinator of Detention Ministry
1357 E. Capitol St., S.E.
Washington, DC 20003

Mrs. Helen Bruns
Archdiocese of Anchorage
225 Cordova St., Building A
Anchorage, AK 99501

Sr. Joan Campbell, S.P.
Archdiocese of San Francisco
445 Church St.
San Francisco, CA 94114

Sr. Mary T. Coffey, S.N.D.
Maine Correction Center
S. Windham, ME 04082

Mr. Kenneth Hofforth
Criminal Justice Coordinator
Catholic Charities Office
1011-1st Ave.
New York, NY 10022

Sr. Suzanne Jabro, C.S.J.
Prison and Jail Ministry
3607-228th Ave., S.E.
Issaquah, WA 98027

Mrs. Carol Johnson
O.P.C.J. Catholic Charities
433 Jefferson St.
Oakland, CA 94607

Fr. Pat Leslie, Chaplain
P.O. Box 2000
Vacaville, CA 95696

Sr. Natalie Rossie, R.S.M.
400 Walter, N.E.
Albuquerque, NM 87102

Sr. Cathy Vallejo, C.S.J.
422 W. Almond
Orange, CA 92666

2) American Catholic Corrections Chaplains Association Officers:

President:
   Sr. Joan Campbell, S.P.
   F.C.I. Pleasanton
   5701 8th St., Camp Parks
   Dublin, CA 94568
   415/829-3522

Vice-President:
   Rev. Felipe S. Maraya
   1204 N. Mesa, Apt. 8
   El Paso, TX 79902
   915/542-1184

Secretary:
   Fr. John Wilkinson
   409 Linden St.
   Brooklyn, NY 11237
   718/520-5287

Treasurer:
Fr. Donald McNally, O.M.I.
P.O. Box 801
Sugarland, TX 77478
713/277-7000

Regions

Breakdown of American Catholic Correctional Chaplains Association into regions, indicating national vice-presidents responsible for each region:

East

Fr. Francis Menei
3509 Spring Garden St.
Philadelphia, PA 19104
215/489-4151

Connecticut, Delaware, District of Columbia, Maine, Maryland, Massachusetts, New Hampshire, New Jersey, New York, Pennsylvania, Rhode Island, Vermont, Virginia, West Virginia.

Central

Fr. Jack Heraty
301 Fifth Ave.
Mooseheart, IL 60539
312/859-2000

Colorado, Illinois, Indiana, Iowa, Kansas, Kentucky, Michigan, Minnesota, Missouri, Nebraska, North Dakota, Ohio, South Dakota, Wisconsin.

Southwest

Fr. Richard Houlahan, O.M.I.
8901 S. Wilmot Rd.
Tucson, AZ 85706
602/795-6649

Arizona, California, Hawaii, Nevada, Utah.

South

Deacon Joe Potter
Texas Dept. of Corrections
Huntsville, TX 77343

Arkansas, Louisiana, Mississippi, New Mexico, Oklahoma, Texas.

Southeast

Fr. Mark Santo
Metropolitan Correction Center/Miami
15801 S.W. 137th Ave.
Miami, FL 33177
305/253-4400

Alabama, Florida, Georgia, North Carolina, South Carolina, Tennessee.

Northwest

Fr. James Jacobson, S.J.
Oregon State Penitentiary
2605 State St.
Salem, OR 97310
503/378-2333

Alaska, Idaho, Montana, Oregon, Washington, Wyoming.

Materials to apply for certification in ACCCA can be obtained from Fr. John Wilkinson, the secretary.

3) Convocation of Jail and Prison Ministers

Fr. Michael Bryant
1357 E. Capitol S.E.
Washington, DC 20003
202/547-1715

Canada
The Rev. Christopher Carr
Associate Director, Chaplaincy and Training
Correctional Service, Canada
340 Laurier Ave. W.
Ottawa, ON K1A 0P9
(613) 996-7749

NHQ
340 Laurier Ave. W.
2nd Floor
Ottawa, ON K1A 0P9
(613) 996-7749

RHQ-Atlantic
Terminal Plaza Building
1222 Main Terminal Building
Moncton, NB F1C 1H6
(506) 857-6392

RHQ-Quebec
3 place Laval, 2nd Floor
Chomedey
Laval, PQ H7N 1A2
(514) 662-3349

RHQ-Ontario
P.O. Box 1174
440 King Street W.
Kingston, ON K7L 4Y8
(613) 545-8690

RHQ-Prairies
P.O. Box 9223
2002 Quebec Ave.
Saskatoon, SK S7K 3X5
(306) 975-4463

RHQ-Pacific
P.O. Box 4500
600-32315 S. Fraser Way
Abbotsford, BC V2T 4M8
(604) 854-2565

Who Am I?

Who am I? . . .
restless and longing and sick, like a bird in a cage,
struggling for breath, as though hands were compressing my
    throat,
hungry for colors, for flowers, for the voices of birds,
thirsty for words of kindness, for neighborliness . . . .

                          —Dietrich Bonhoeffer